PENTAGRAM RITUAL

THE ESSENTIAL SKILLS OF MAGICK

TARQUIN NEVERTHORNE

The Three Essential Skills

All effective magick stands on three legs: imagination, emotion, and feeling; everything else – all the words and gestures, the implements and costumes, the elaborate circles and furniture – serve only to reinforce and focus these three capacities. If any of these three is lacking, then the work is likely to fail; once you are skilled in using all three, you can dispense with practically all the other things people sometimes insist are essential to the practice. Of the three, emotion is the power that drives the whole show; emotion from the guts, and from the heart. I will go even further; it is not just emotion, but *passion* that is the power behind magick. Passion in the sense of an intense desire to be connected to that which you are seeking to invoke; a desire that places no restrictions or limits on the connection, but which is so one-pointed that nothing save that which is sought is included within its focus. And passion in the sense of a boundless enthusiasm for the acts by which you seek to create that connection. Admittedly, this is the ideal case; but the closer you can get to it, even for a few moments, the more likely your work is to be successful. This passion-for-connection is what creates the *magickal link* between the magician and that which he is invoking; or, if the link already exists, expands it and strengthens it. The emotion literally creates a channel or umbilicus between them, through which energy and knowledge can flow in either

4

direction. The stronger the emotion, the stronger the link becomes; the less energy is lost in side-thoughts and distractions, the stronger the link becomes. Thus a one-pointed focus is most desireable. But conversely, restrictions the magician places on the connection become constrictions in the link, reducing the potential flow of power through it. If a magician insists that a spiritual force or being manifest itself in a specific way, then it is less likely to appear, or the manifestation with be weaker. But if his desire for connection is *unconditional*, then a response is much more likely, and will be more powerful when it comes. Similarly, if a magician doing a ritual to obtain money desires that money to appear in the form of a cashier's check, he is less likely to obtain it than if he was willing to accept it in any form. In its highest form, this unconditional passion becomes almost indistinguishable from what is called "Divine Love", which is the closest that one can come (within the worlds of manifestation) to the transcendental state of the Mother aspect of divinity. Passion-for-connection transforms into a state of pure *relationship*, pure Love, in which all distinctions are erased; both the nature of the magician and the nature of that being invoked disappear, totally lost in the link between them. Imagination provides the medium (rather, an opening to the medium) through which magick produces its results. The personal imagination seems to blend seamlessly into the astral light, the larger magickal universe; the point at which one becomes the other is impossible to define clearly. An object that begins as a purely internal construct – created and sustained by the imagination of a magician, propelled by the power of emotion – can move out into the astral light and take on a life independent of its creator. It can gather or become a container for magickal power, and act back on its creator (or on others) in ways that are impossible for him to produce through his imagination alone. Conversely, beings and powers operating on levels the magician cannot yet perceive can make themselves known to the him through his receptive imagination, opening his awareness into new realms of experience. The symbols used in magick are forms that, when created in the imagination, tend to gather specific types of power from the astral light, which are further limited by the intent of the magician. The shape of the container, in effect, determines what can be put into it; the simpler, rigidly geometric forms (such as the pentagram and hexagram) draw relatively pure, fundamental forces; complex symbols – e.g., god-forms – draw correspondingly complex assemblages of forces. When the magician projects the image of a symbol onto his surroundings, an extended magickal space is created in which the astral light becomes conditioned into conformity with the symbol. The area becomes more attractive

6

to the types of power invoked, more comfortable for magickal beings having the nature represented by the symbol. The world of the powers and the world of the magician then intersect, making interaction possible. (A detailed series of practices for developing the imagination and creating a general-purpose magickal space can be found in my article *A Short Course in Scrying*. This present paper is aimed towards showing by example how it is used in formal rituals.) Feeling is the third leg of the tripod, and the final key to success in magick. In order to bring into being the conditions you desire, you must create in yourself the sensations and feelings that the things you have created through your imagination are real, and that *the goal of the operation has already been accomplished*. In the magickal universe, when you act with all your being as if something is already real, it becomes real. This feeling of reality is the trigger that causes a symbol to move from the imagination into the astral light. This key to magick is simply stated, but in practice it seems to give the greatest difficulty for most people. The usual culprits are intellectual doubts – "I know I am only imagining this" – and fears of various sorts, e.g., "what if it makes me go crazy?" Both of these have to be ruthlessly eliminated from the magician's consciousness for the duration of the operation. After the work is completely over, you can be as doubtful and fear-ridden as you want; a certain amount of doubt, of critical examination, is healthy and appropriate at that time. But during the work, you must be completely focused on feeling (*not* thinking) that what you create is real. Some might be concerned that this "believing makes it real" idea is actually a form of self-hypnosis, a way of fooling oneself by reducing the critical faculties. A genuine success in performing the ritual will dispose of this concern. At some point in the work a threshold is crossed; the strength of the invocation produces an even stronger response from somewhere outside yourself. Events in your magickal space take on a life of their own, at least partially independent of your will. And – most significant – they begin to manifest an intensity, richness and texture that it is utterly impossible for you to produce through your imagination alone, no matter how adept you might be in its use. Once this has been experienced even a skeptical mind must grant that the events are "real" in some sense, even if not in the same way as mundane happenings. So for magick to be successful, emotion must push a link outwards into the magickal universe, imagination must aim it towards the desired goal, and feeling must affirm the reality of that which is sought. Full success will not come on the first try; for some people, not even on the fiftieth. It takes time to condition the mind to the proper performance of these practices. But once a single success is attained, additional successes follow at more frequent intervals.

The Golden Dawn's Pentagram Ritual

The Pentagram Ritual is an excellent practice-piece for developing proficiency in these three essential skills. Its physical and verbal elements are simple and easily memorized, enabling the student to give most of his attention to the visualizations and the feelings attending them. But for all its simplicity, it is capable of producing profound effects on the consciousness of the magician. Performing it is also of long-term benefit; it purifies and strengthens the magician's magickal body, and increases his general sensitivity to events in the magickal universe. Oddly, the most frequently referenced descriptions of the Pentagram Ritual make almost no mention of its imagery and feeling components. Perhaps in the Golden Dawn and Crowley's A\A\, these were expected to be the subject of verbal instruction, or were simply assumed to be too obvious to mention. Regardless, it was the absence of such descriptions that prompted a student to request the elaborated version of the ritual that follows. The Pentagram is a symbol whose power is partly innate, and partly a matter of the magician's intent. Its natural tendency (in the astral light) is to attract a dynamic, active mix of the elemental forces; in contrast, the equalarmed cross attracts the same forces but tends to keep them fixed and distinct from each other. But when the Pentagram is used to invoke a specific element, the element is determined largely by the magician's habitual methods of usage and his intent of the moment. There are several methods of encoding the desired element in the way the Pentagram is drawn; all of these are more or less arbitrary, and depend on *consistent use and practice* to be effective.

Figure 1.

In modern magickal systems, it is customary to associate the elements with the points of the Pentagram as shown in Figure 1. This set of associations derives from the Golden Dawn, and was intended to reflect the positions of the Elemental Tablets within the "Revised" Great Table of the Enochian magickal system. Had they chosen to use the original version of the Great Table (as would seem more appropriate, from more recent research) a substantially different set of associations would result: Earth would be at the upper right point, Water at the lower right, and Fire at the lower left. Since the Golden Dawn associations have come into general usage, it seems convenient to stay with them. The method of drawing invoking and banishing Pentagrams is also arbitrary, and in this case, the Golden Dawn used a method that is cumbersome, difficult to remember, and contains an undesirable dualism. To replace it, I recommend the method used by the Aurum Solis, which is simple and self-consistent. To draw an invoking Pentagram, draw clockwise from the point associated with the desired element; to draw a banishing Pentagram, draw counterclockwise from the same point. In the Golden Dawn version of the ritual, the magician is instructed to draw a pentagram of Earth in every quarter. The theory behind this was that the element of Earth serves as container or receptacle for the other three elements. This idea seems to derive from an old interpretation in which Fire, Water, and Air were the true elements, and Earth merely something on which they acted. I feel it more appropriate to use the pentagram of Spirit. Spirit contains all the other elements within itself on an equal basis, and facilitates the transformations between them that make possible activity and life in the manifest world; it is more truly "generic".

The Lesser Ritual of the Pentagram

The Opening.

1. Stand in the center of the circle, feet together, facing east. Using your thumb, touch the center of your forehead, and vibrate "**Ateh**." *As you say "Ateh," imagine a beam of light coming down from the heavens, and forming a sphere or dome of brilliant white light, about nine inches across, above your head. Note: Wherever a glowing sphere, column, or line is mentioned it should appear like a neon light, transparent or translucent with every point of its interior emanating light. Your body should be perfectly "transparent" to all these images; that is, the lines and column should pass through your body without being hindered by it in any way.*

2. Still using your thumb, gesture slowly down the centerline of your body until your thumb is pointing at the ground between your feet. *As your gesture moves downwards, imagine a column of white light about 3 inches thick, descending from the sphere through the center of your body at the same rate of speed (as if you were "drawing" the column with your gesture). Feel the column as being filled with a vibrating energy that sets up a sympathetic vibration in your body wherever it passes.* Vibrate "**Malkuth**." *Imagine the column of light descending into the ground below your feet. Once there, it anchors itself in place and forms another ball of light; this ball starts out a dark red,*

*but quickly becomes brighter and whiter as more
energy feeds into it.*

3. Touch your right arm at the level of your
heart and vibrate "**ve- Geburah**." *Imagine a
small sphere of light forming where you touch.*
Move your hand horizontally to the same point
on your left arm and vibrate "**ve-Gedulah**." *As
you move your hand, imagine another line of white
light being traced horizontally through the center of
your body, intersecting the vertical column about
where your heart is. When the line reaches your left
arm, imagine another small ball of light forming
there. Then imagine a flow of energy back and forth
between them. Feel that energy as it passes through
your body, and begins to produce a tingling
sensation in your heart.*

4. Make a clockwise circle about 6" across
around your heart. Vibrate "**le- Olahm**." *As
soon as you complete this circle, imagine a big pink
rose blooming inside it, with its stem at the
intersection of the horizontal and vertical lines of the
cross. Feel the movements of its petals in your heart
as it unfolds. When it is completely unfolded,
imagine a rose-pink radiance being emitted from it
in all directions. This radiance expands until it
completely encloses the cross and your body.*

5. Vibrate "**Amen**." Bring your arms down to
your sides, relax as much as you can while still
standing straight, and take a few moments to

appreciate and feel everything that you have visualized so far. You should generate in yourself a sense of satisfaction with what you have done so far, and joy in the result.

6. Let the above visualizations fade. Don't try to "erase" them, just stop giving attention to their maintenance. If they continue to exist without any effort on your part, that's fine. If they disappear, that's fine, too. **Main Ceremony.**

7. Advance to the east point of the circle. Draw a large pentagram with your wand, or with the pointed fingers of your hand. *The lines of all the pentagrams, and the circle connecting them, should be seen in a blue-white color. They should have a perceptible, three-dimensional thickness, at least equal to that of a clothesline or thin rope.* Make a stabbing gesture at the center of the pentagram with wand or hand, and vibrate "**Yahweh.**" *As you vibrate the name, imagine the inside of the pentagram becoming an open window into the Realms of Air. Beyond the window, you should imagine some landscape that seems Airy to you. One image works especially well for me: the view from a Tuscan hill town, the sky an almost painfully brilliant blue, creating a dome so vast and seemingly deep that it dwarfs all the human and natural features of the landscape into insignificance. The "Big Sky" of the American Plains is a similar image. Whatever, you should feel that the landscape is filled to overflowing with the force of Air, vast in extent,*

17

*all-penetrating, and etherial. Imagine that this realm
extends to infinity in the direction you are facing.
Once you have the landscape firmly visualized,
imagine a cool wind blowing into your circle
through the pentagram. Feel the wind filling up the
circle and blowing through your body and soul,
leaving no part of you untouched. It blows out and
replaces the impure Airy elements of your own
nature with pure Airy power. Keep feeling this wind
until you feel cleaned out and filled with Airy
power. Note: If you are banishing, you should next
feel the power sweeping out of yourself and the
circle, back through the pentagram. After which you
should imagine the "window" closing again. Same
for all the following quarters. Take a few moments to
stop and appreciate whatever degree of Airyness you
have managed to bring into the circle. Feel a sense of
satisfaction with it, and vow to make it even better
the next time. Then stop consciously supporting the
images and feelings. At first they will fade, but with
continued practice you will find that a residual
feeling of the element will remain in the circle
throughout the rest of the ceremony.*

8. Move clockwise around the circle until you
come to the south. Starting at the center of the
eastern pentagram, draw a blue-white line as
you go. Face the south and draw a large
pentagram. Make the stabbing gesture at the
center of the pentagram, and vibrate "**Adonai**."
*Imagine the pentagram opening into the Realms of
Fire. The landscape you choose should present a*

feeling of intense, radiant heat, like that you feel on your face from the Sun, only sourceless and omnidirectional. An appropriate image might be Death Valley at noon, with shimmering waves of heat filling space in all directions. Or the surface of the Sun -- ultimate, incandescent heat. The landscape should feel full to bursting with the power of the element, and feel like it extends to infinity in the direction you are facing. When the landscape has been firmly established, feel the heat rushing into your circle through the pentagram. Feel it filling the circle and yourself, burning out any impurities and totally consuming them, then replacing them with pure Fiery force. Continue until you feel completely purified by the Fire and filled with its force. Take a few moments to stop and appreciate whatever degree of Fieryness you have managed to bring into the circle. Feel a sense of satisfaction with it, and vow to make it even better the next time. Then stop consciously supporting the images and feelings.

9. Move clockwise to the west, drawing a segment of the circle as you go. Face the west, and draw a large pentagram. Make the stabbing gesture at the center of the pentagram, and vibrate "**Eheieh**." *Imagine the pentagram becoming a window into the Realms of Water. Imagine a watery landscape. I use either an infinite region filled with water of a deep, almost violet blue color; or an underwater view of a reef with plenty of fish and plant life, and waves crossing the surface overhead. With the landscape visualized, imagine*

Water gushing into the circle and yourself, dissolving any impurities and diluting them into nothingness, replacing them with its own pure power. Keep feeling this until you feel clean and totally filled with Water. Pause to appreciate the Watery element you have managed to bring into the circle. Feel satisfaction with it, and know that you can do even more the next time. Then stop consciously supporting the images.

10. Move clockwise to the north, drawing the circle as you go. Face the north, draw a large pentagram. Make the stabbing gesture at the center of the pentagram and vibrate "**AGLA**." *Imagine the pentagram becoming a window into the Realms of Earth, beyond which you can see some landscape that seems supremely "Earthy" to you. I use either a soft, warm darkness of infinite extent; a cave with ancient paintings on the walls; or cultivated land with all sorts of food-crops growing. The emphasis should be on the* fertility *and potential for life hidden in the darkness of the Earth, rather than the view of Earth as cold, sterile stone. Imagine the Earthy power moving through the pentagram, filling up the circle and penetrating your body, making any impurities so inert and heavy that they fall downwards out of your body, to be replaced by a pure earth force. Keep feeling this until you feel clean and totally filled with Earth. As in the preceding quarters, pause to appreciate the Earthy element you have managed to bring into the circle. Feel satisfaction with it, and know that you*

can do even more the next time. Then stop
consciously supporting the images.

11. Complete the circle by returning clockwise
to the east, drawing the line as you go. Return
to the center of the circle and face east. *Standing
in the center of the circle, try to see all four
landscapes at once, and feel the power of all four
elements focused on you through the pentagrams.*

12. Say: "**Before me stands Raphael; behind
me stands Gabriel; on my right hand is
Michael; on my left hand is Auriel.**" The
names of the archangels should be vibrated. *The
angels should be imagined appearing as their names
are vibrated. Each should be seen as an immense
figure on the horizon beyond the landscape in their
quarter. You should have a definite sense of them as
sapient, self-aware beings of great power, come to
aid you in your work. The landscapes represent the
natural, non-sapient force of the elements; the
archangels represent the divine powers that rule and
direct those elements. The archangels should have
some form that signifies – in your mind – their
rulership over their elements. I see them as figures in
robes the color of their elements. Raphael has blond
hair that moves in an invisible breeze; he holds a fan
or dagger in his right hand pointed towards you. His
face has an aquiline cast. Gabriel has dark hair with
a bluish cast, dark skin, and holds a silver cup
towards you. His robes seem to move in an invisible
current. Michael has hair and eyes like flames, a*

21

slightly fox-like cast to his face, and his robes seem to be made of woven threads of fire. He holds a flaming sword pointed towards you. Auriel wears black or green robes. His face is rounded, and of a nut-brown color. He holds a disk-like pantacle with one face pointed towards you. Imagine each of the archangels sending a benediction to you through his weapon.

13. Stand with your arms stretched out to the sides, and feet apart. Say: "**About me flame the pentagrams...**" *See the four pentagrams and the lines connecting them suddenly flaring to an intense brightness around you. As they do so, imagine a fifth, equally bright pentagram forming about your body, its points congruent with your head, hands, and feet. Remember that the pentagram signifies rulership of the Spirit over the four elements, and that by identifying it you are claiming that rulership for yourself. Try to feel yourself as Spirit, connected to the four elements, but also above them.* Say: "**...and in the column shines the six-rayed star!**" *Your mood as you say these words should be one of triumph and exultation, a sense of complete success in the endeavor of invoking the elements. Imagine a large golden hexagram, the same width as your circle, forming in the air above you. Rays of power shine radially outwards from each of its points. The lowest point of the hexagram is congruent with the highest point of the pentagram previously visualized. The hexagram signifies the planetary or "heavenly" realms that are above the*

worlds of the elements. *Elemental Spirit is a summation or concentration of these heavenly forces. By claiming the power of the elemental Spirit, you are also declaring your freedom from the rule of the mundane world, and claiming the right to enter into and work in those higher realms.*

The Response.

14. At this point, the invocation is effectively complete. You have finished setting up the conditions for a response from the astral light; now you must give that response a chance to occur. This is an utterly vital part of any invocation you will ever do; you may get some response while performing the ritual, but the most important, the most vital, revealing, and consciousness- expanding part of the response nearly always takes place in the quiet time after the active work has ended.

You should now cease all active visualizations, and assume a relaxed, comfortable position, standing or sitting. Silently open yourself to the forces you have invoked, *listen* for them with your mind, your body, and your aura. Don't *do* anything, and don't *think* about doing anything for a time; just absorb your magickal environment as passively as a "couch potato" watching TV.

When it seems, after a while, as if everything that is going to occur has occurred, do the ceremonial closing to complete the session.

The Closing

15. Repeat the "Cabalistic Cross" from steps 1 through 6.

22390511R00016

Printed in Great Britain
by Amazon